DALE EARNHARDT JR. *Stats*

Cars:

Sikkens No. 31 Chevy (1st Busch Grand National)
AC Delco No. 3 (2nd and main Busch Grand National)
Budweiser No. 8 Chevy (Winston Cup)

Major Wins:

7 (Winston Cup), 15 (Busch Grand National)
• May 20, 2000 — The Winston Winner

Earnings

$13,382,494 (Winston Cup)
$3,187,954 (Busch Grand National)

Poles:

6 (Winston Cup)
8 (Busch Grand National)

Top 5 Finishes:

23 (Winston Cup)
36 (Busch Grand National)

Top 10 Finishes:

37 (Winston Cup)
47 (Busch Grand National)

Championships:

1998 and 1999 Busch Grand National Championship

Teams:

Dale Earnhardt Inc. (DEI)

Sponsors:

Remington Arms, Nabisco, Drakkar Noir, The Outlaw, Coca-Cola,
Snap-On Tools, Food-City and Chevrolet.

Fun Facts:

Began driving as a professional at 17. He diversified one step further in 2001
when he competed in the Rolex 24 at Daytona, driving a factory-prepared
Chevrolet Corvette with Earnhardt Sr.

DALE EARNHARDT JR.

JUNIOR ACHIEVEMENT:
The Dale Earnhardt Jr. Story

TRIUMPH
BOOKS
CHICAGO

Author:
David Poole

Photography:
The Charlotte Observer

Editor:
Constance Holloway

Design Team:
Larry Preslar
Beth Epperly
Andrea Ross

This book is a joint production of Triumph Books and the New Ventures Division of Knight Publishing Co.

This book is available in quantity at special discounts for your group or organization. For further information, contact:

Triumph Books
601 South LaSalle Street, Suite 500
Chicago, Illinois 60605
(312) 939-3330
Fax (312) 663-3557

Printed in the United States of America

ISBN 1-57243-551-8

David Poole has covered NASCAR for The Charlotte (N.C.) Observer since 1997. He has won awards for his coverage from the Associated Press Sports Editors and the National Motorsports Press Association. He was the winner of the George Cunningham Award as the NMPA's writer of the year in 2001. Poole is a graduate of the University of North Carolina and lives in his hometown of Gastonia, N.C., with his wife, Karen, and her three children, Matthew, David and Emily.

TABLE OF CONTENTS

Chapter 1
He's an Earnhardt 7

Chapter 2
A Legend in the Making 12

Chapter 3
Championship Caliber 18

Chapter 4
A World to Conquer 22

Chapter 5
Giant Steps 26

Chapter 6
Farewell, Superman 32

Chapter 7
Like Father, Like Son 38

Chapter 8
The Need to Succeed 42

EARNHARDT

he's an

"Earn-hardt! Earn-hardt! Earn-hardt!"

Thousands of fans at Lowe's Motor Speedway were chanting his name in unison, and Dale Earnhardt Jr. was looking around to see whom they were calling for.

"Earn-hardt! Earn-hardt! Earn-hardt!"

Earnhardt Jr. had heard the chant dozens of times before. He'd been there, not always but some of the times, when race fans shouted as one in praise of his father, seven-time NASCAR Winston Cup champion Dale Earnhardt.

This time, though, things were different.

The date was May 20, 2000, and minutes earlier The Winston all-star race had just wrapped up in thrilling fashion. An Earnhardt had roared from the back of the pack to the front in the final eight laps, taking the checkered flag in an event that had, from its inception, seemed to be custom-designed to fit the Earnhardt driving style.

"Earn-hardt! Earn-hardt! Earn-hardt!"

The fans kept on chanting, and Earnhardt Jr. kept on looking around. Even though he knew they were cheering for him.

"It was kind of funny for me to stand there and hear people cheering, 'Earn-hardt! Earn-hardt! Earn-hardt!' when I'm the only Earnhardt standing up there," Earnhardt Jr. would say that night, soon after becoming the first Winston Cup rookie to win The Winston. "That was kind of weird."

Over the ensuing few years, Earnhardt Jr. would get more used to the cheers. Tragically, he would also soon begin shouldering more of the burden of carrying the family name into NASCAR's future than anyone could have ever imagined on that night.

Growing up an Earnhardt isn't the easiest thing in the world anyway. Being

Being Dale Earnhardt Jr. is especially tough, because the original was, well, an absolute, one-of-a-kind original.

Dale Earnhardt Jr. is especially tough, because the original was, well, an absolute, one-of-a-kind original.

Dale Earnhardt grew up as the son of a famous race car driver, too. His father, Ralph, was one of the greatest short-track racers to ever turn a steering wheel, and his son Dale idolized him. Dale would wake up in the morning after Ralph had raced on some dirt track the night before and run out to look at the car. He could almost always tell how things had gone with one look — if the car was anywhere close to in one piece, Ralph had most likely brought home a little money from the track.

Dale wanted to be just like his father, but Ralph wanted his son to get at least a high school education. Ralph knew how hard it could be to make a decent living driving a race car, and wanted Dale to have at least a fighting chance in life if that didn't work out for him. Dale, though, was in a big hurry to go racing and wouldn't listen to Ralph. Dale quit school and Ralph didn't like it one bit.

Dale and Ralph had patched things up before Ralph died of a heart attack at age 45, and as the years passed Dale learned more and more each day just how smart his father had really been.

"I should have listened to my dad better," Earnhardt said. "That's the main lesson in life. Everything he told me came out to be true. Why did I not believe him? I wish I'd have listened better to the basic things he taught me."

Van Camp's
BEANS
nington
ARMS
CINCINNATI
weiser
8
SPORT
CINCINNATI
FIRE DIVISION

"I've told Dale Jr. the same thing. I said, 'You're not going to believe me or listen to me, but this is what I learned from my dad and it all came true.' I'm giving him advice the best I can."

There were times when it seemed Earnhardt Jr. wasn't listening at all. But by the time he'd made it to Winston Cup, NASCAR's top circuit, it was apparent to anyone paying attention that, at least when it came to racing, Earnhardt Jr. had learned his lessons well.

His father had tied Richard Petty's all-time record by winning seven championships. He'd won every major race there is in the sport, completing the resume with an emotional victory in the 1998 Daytona 500, and had turned his "The Intimidator" image into a public persona and a marketing bonanza.

Earnhardt Jr. has his father's name. In his first three seasons in Winston Cup racing, he has also shown that he has at least some of his father's skills, especially in solving the mysteries of racing at Daytona and Talladega, the sport's biggest two tracks.

He is not, however, his father.

Earnhardt wore dark sunglasses and hung out with country musicians. Earnhardt Jr. wears his baseball caps backward and dresses in baggy blue jeans and T-shirts like some of the musicians in the rock 'n' roll bands whose music he loves. Earnhardt Jr. surfs the Internet, while the only computer Earnhardt ever mastered was the one that gave him an unmatched seat-of-the-pants feel while driving a race car.

As different as they could be, though, there are also striking similarities. Foremost among those is how Earnhardt Sr. and Earnhardt Jr. both represent a bridge across two distinct eras in what is today America's fastest growing sport.

Earnhardt started his career on the red-clay dirt tracks in the Carolinas, the tracks where Ralph Earnhardt raced so well he earned a spot among the 50 greatest drivers in NASCAR history. Over the course of his career, he helped propel stock-car racing from those roots into the mainstream of America's professional sports psyche, becoming in fact its most recognizable icon.

Earnhardt Jr. stepped into NASCAR's elite just as the sport was beginning to climb its next mountain, becoming a star just as Winston Cup racing moved from cable to network television and just as his father's generation of superstars was heading into its final years of competitive racing. NASCAR was going nationwide, expanding its appeal to a younger, hipper audience.

So far, he has been up to the challenge. Earnhardt Jr. is, perhaps, the closest thing stock-car racing has ever had to a true rock star. And he's a one heck of a race car driver, too.

Of course, that much we already knew.

"He's an Earnhardt," his father once said.

A LEGEND
in the making

Dale Earnhardt Jr. was born Oct. 10, 1974, in Kannapolis, the small North Carolina textile mill town where his grandfather and father had both put down the family's roots.

His mother, Brenda, was Dale Earnhardt's second wife and also is the mother of Earnhardt Jr.'s older sister, Kelley. His half-brother, Kerry, was five years older.

Both of Earnhardt's first two marriages ended in divorce, in part because of the demands placed upon a young man trying to balance supporting a family with the cost of pursuing a career in auto racing.

Earnhardt Jr. lived with his mother until just after he started school, but as his father began to enjoy success in Winston Cup in the early 1980s,

Earnhardt regained custody of Kelley and Earnhardt Jr.

Earnhardt had quit school after the ninth grade to go racing, a decision that angered his father, Ralph, and Earnhardt grew to regret both his decision to leave school and the rift it caused between himself and his father. He made it clear to his children that he expected them to get their high school diplomas.

Earnhardt Jr. did that from Mooresville High in 1992, where he played soccer as well, then spent two years studying at a trade school before getting a job at his father's Chevrolet dealership in Newton, N.C. Earnhardt Jr. changed oil, hammered out dents and did whatever he was asked to do to help out.

Things were not always perfect between Earnhardt Jr. and his dad.

It's hard for a race car driver named Earnhardt to fly under the radar for long.

Earnhardt Jr. spent the seventh and eighth grades at Oak Hill Military Academy in Greensboro in an effort to curb his rambunctious side. He also would later say he resented the fact that his father, who'd been the one insisting he complete high school, missed his graduation ceremony because he was off at a race track.

Their common ground, however, was racing.

Earnhardt Jr. had worked at odd jobs around his father's race shop, learning bit by bit about the family business. He eventually built a red Chevrolet Monte Carlo that, at age 17, he began driving in street stock division races at Concord Motorsport Park, not far from Kannapolis.

"If you pay attention, that's where you get good at what you do," Earnhardt Jr. would say later.

He also raced Legends cars at Charlotte Motor Speedway, half-scale replicas of coupes and sedans from the 1930s and '40s that sold then for about $8,500.

At the Charlotte track in October 1992, the night before his 18th birthday, Earnhardt Jr. scooted onto the infield grass off Turn 4 on the final lap of a 25-lap race and then bumped Hank Jones, a member of his dad's pit crew and the owner of the car Earnhardt Jr. was driving, out of the way to get his first win.

"I reckon that's the way it goes," Earnhardt Jr. said.

He shared a desire to race with his brother and sister, and in 1994 Earnhardt helped each of them get a shot at running in the late model division on one of the short tracks around the Carolinas.

Kerry would run at Hickory Motor Speedway, the historic track where his dad and grandfather had cut their competitive teeth, with Kelley running at Caraway Speedway in Asheboro and at Concord. Earnhardt Jr., meanwhile, would spend the year chasing the track championship at Myrtle Beach Speedway in South Carolina.

Kelley, who was then a senior at UNC-Charlotte, would eventually give up racing while Kerry continues trying to get his career on the fast track.

Earnhardt Jr., however, was on his way. He didn't dominate at the Myrtle Beach track, but as he continued to learn more and more about his race cars he was also having the time of his life. He raced with a group of guys he considered his friends and spent time with them on South Carolina's "Grand Strand" when they weren't at the track.

Things would begin to get more serious soon enough, however. He made his

first career start in NASCAR's Busch Series when it visited Myrtle Beach on June 22, 1996, finishing 14th.

It's hard for a race car driver named Earnhardt to fly under the radar for long. People began to take notice of the young man who'd so far managed to quietly gain experience, confidence and — perhaps most critically — his father's trust.

In 1997, Dale Earnhardt Inc. put a driver from New York state named Steve Park into a car in the Grand National series. Park won rookie-of-the-year honors in that series and when Earnhardt decided that DEI was ready to make the leap into full-time Winston Cup competition the following season, he decided Park was the driver to do it with.

That left an opening in the team's Busch Series ride, an opening that Earnhardt decided his younger son was ready to fill.

Earnhardt Jr.'s career in NASCAR's big-time was about to get the green flag.

CHAMPIONSHIP *caliber*

Earnhardt Jr. dipped his toes into the ocean of NASCAR's Busch Series in 1996 and 1997. In 1998, he waded right in.

His rookie season began at Daytona in February, and he qualified third fastest for the NAPA 300. Considering how famous his father had made that No. 3, it seemed like a good omen.

Perhaps not.

He ran in the top five until an early pit stop, when he came in too fast and slid past his pit stall. His jack man had to jump and roll across the hood to avoid being run over, and when Earnhardt Jr. tried to back into position he tore the drive shaft out of his Chevrolet.

Earnhardt Jr. lost nearly 20 laps as his team made repairs, but his troubles weren't over. Later in the race, Earnhardt

Jr.'s car got tapped from behind on the backstretch by Dick Trickle's. Earnhardt Jr.'s Chevy rose into the air and began twisting, landing on Trickle's car before coming to rest against the inside guardrail.

One year earlier, his father had taken an eerily similar tumble down the backstretch in the Daytona 500. Earnhardt had climbed into, then out of an ambulance and drove his black No. 3 back to pit road. Earnhardt Jr. didn't do that, but he did shrug off the crash.

"I banged my head around a little," he said. "It's not really that scary. It's just something that's going to happen and it happened today.'"

Good things started happening for Earnhardt Jr. just a few weeks later. The Busch Series rookie won his first pole at

"I want to thank my dad for everything he's done for me, supporting me through my life, putting me through school, giving me a good education and helping me get an opportunity to drive race cars. He's helped me fulfill my dream."

Bristol in March and finished second in the race to Elliott Sadler.

Earnhardt Jr. carried that momentum to Texas Motor Speedway the next time out, and with one lap to go in the Coca-Cola 300 he was right on leader Joe Nemechek's back bumper.

Coming off Turn 4, Earnhardt Jr. used his fresher tires to dive to the inside of Nemechek. Just past the white flag, Earnhardt Jr. got the lead. Sadler chased the new leader hard on the final lap and got within a car-length, but couldn't deny Earnhardt Jr. his first career Busch Series victory.

His father, who'd been coaching Earnhardt Jr. over the radio, was there when the winner pulled into victory lane. They exchanged hugs before Earnhardt Jr. got out of his car.

"That was pretty awesome, wasn't it?" Earnhardt said.

After wrecking three times in a four-race stretch later that spring, Earnhardt

Jr. won again at Dover at the end of May. He won again at Milwaukee in July, leading 208 of 250 laps, then took the points lead from Matt Kenseth with another dominant win at California Speedway two weeks later. After getting a penalty for a bumping incident at South Boston, Va., the next weekend, he won again at Indianapolis Raceway Park. He led 236 of 250 laps and held off Winston Cup stars Jimmy Spencer and Jeff Burton to win again at Richmond, solidifying his points lead.

In October, in the 28th of the season's 31 races, Earnhardt Jr. won again at Gateway near St. Louis and padded his lead to 102 points. When he got to Homestead-Miami Speedway for the season's final race, all he had to do was take the green flag to clinch his first Busch Series title. He wrecked in practice and blew an engine in the race, finishing 42nd. It didn't matter. He held off Kenseth by 48 points and brought home a champi-

onship for his father's race team.

"'I guess it will sink in once I see the look in my daddy's eyes," Earnhardt Jr. had said before the final race. "I want to thank my dad for everything he's done for me, supporting me through my life, putting me through school, giving me a good education and helping me get an opportunity to drive race cars. He's helped me fulfill my dream."

Tony Eury Jr., Earnhardt Jr.'s cousin, had grown up side by side and Tony's father, Tony Sr. had at times been like a second father when the elder Earnhardt was off writing his own racing legend. When Earnhardt started a Busch team at DEI, he make Eury Sr. the crew chief and Tony Jr. were on the crew.

"We knew (Earnhardt Jr.) had talent," Eury Sr. said. "His daddy came to me about the middle of last year when he decided he was going to put Steve Park in a Cup car. He said, 'You think you can make something out of Dale Jr.?'"

"I said, 'I don't know, but I'll see what I can do.' Well, now I'll take all the credit."

Earnhardt Jr.'s success as a Busch Series rookie had one-upped his father, who'd won Winston Cup rookie-of-the-year honors in 1979, then his first championship the following year. His star was rising rapidly in stock-car racing circles, and his future was quickly taking shape.

In September, Earnhardt Jr. rode into a news conference at the DEI headquarters in Mooresville, on a wagon being pulled by eight Clydesdale horses. He'd signed a contract to go Winston Cup racing with Budweiser beer as his primary sponsor, beginning with five races in 1999 and continuing with a full season in Cup in 2000.

"Things are happening so early in my career," Earnhardt Jr. said. "For someone to take a chance on a young driver like me means so much. ... Everybody's taking a risk here. That's obvious. But I think I'm capable of doing what they want."

a world TO CONQUER

Daytona had provided a rough start for his rookie season, and things didn't go much — at first — better in his sopho- more season.

As happy as he was to win the Busch Series title in 1998, the highlight of that year for Dale Earnhardt Jr. came after the season had ended half a world away from home.

"When I was a little kid, watching my father race…I never sat there saying, 'I want to win the Busch Series champi- onship one day,'" Earnhardt Jr. said. "I said, 'I want the chance to race against him.' As long as I can remember, racing against him was always a dream."

Not even a child's imagination, howev- er, could have pictured that the first on- track meeting between Earnhardt and Earnhardt Jr. would happen in Japan.

In November 1998, the Earnhardts were among a group of drivers traveling to the Orient to participate in NASCAR's third annual exhibition race in Japan. The site for that third race was a gleaming new facility called Twin Ring

Motegi, more than an hour's drive into the mountains from Tokyo.

Earnhardt Jr. was so excited about the opportunity to fulfill that childhood dream that he said the first day of prac- tice at the Motegi track was more excit- ing than winning the Busch Series title. Earnhardt raised his eyebrows at the remark, and also laughed when he was kidded about the fact that the son's fastest lap had been faster than the father's.

Their competitive banter was nothing new. There were two fish mounted on a plaque at the Dale Earnhardt Inc. head- quarters back in Mooresville, N.C. One was the first big crappie Earnhardt Jr. ever caught, the other was one his father caught the same day on Lake Norman. One fish was slightly bigger than the other, and they'd argued for years about who caught which fish.

Earnhardt Jr. outqualified his father, sixth fastest to eighth, and they finished in the same two positions in the Japan race that Mike Skinner won. The Earnhardts' presence in the exhibition provided merely a first glimpse of what it would be like the following year as Earnhardt Jr. tried to defend his Busch Series title and also get in his first five Winston Cup races.

Daytona had provided a rough start for his rookie season, and things didn't go much better in his sophomore season. Earnhardt Jr. wrecked in his first start in the International Race of Champions, a race his father won, then crashed his primary car in the final Busch Series practice session. He then wrecked the backup car in the season's first race the following day.

It would be a while before things got better. Earnhardt Jr. tried to keep his mind on racing the Busch car as the days began to count down toward his first

Winston Cup start, but there were things even an Earnhardt couldn't control.

His debut was planned for the Coca-Cola 600 at Lowe's Motor Speedway in Charlotte, basically a home game for the Kannapolis native, at the end of May. As he raced through the spring without much success, he couldn't keep from looking ahead toward that date, one that everyone around him was making into such a big deal.

"What if we run like crap and the big old promotion gets blown out of the water?" he said. "I am worried about that. Everybody else won't admit it, but I am. You can't help but worry about that at night when you try to go to sleep."

In March, he complained in a Sports Illustrated interview about all the demands being placed on him with a schedule that included up to 70 personal appearances in addition to his Busch and Winston Cup racing commitments. "You can't do anything without thinking

about it...and dreading that life will never be like it was," he said. "A lot of advantages and rewards come with this, but you're so busy you don't have time to enjoy it. So sometimes you wonder, what good is it?"

Earnhardt Jr. handled the pressure. He qualified eighth fastest, matching the car number on the side of his Chevrolet Monte Carlo, and finished three laps down to winner Jeff Burton in 16th position.

With the Cup debut behind him, it was as though Earnhardt Jr. had shed a burden. The next weekend, he got his first Busch Series victory of the '99 season and passed Matt Kenseth for the points lead. He won again the next weekend at South Boston, Va., then made it three straight on the road course at Watkins Glen, N.Y.

During that stretch of racing in June, he also lived out the next chapter of his dreams of racing against his father. In the

third IROC race of the season at Michigan Speedway, Earnhardt Jr. came off Turn 4 on the final lap on the outside of his father, racing him for the victory. They traded bumps through the final stretch, with Earnhardt holding on to win by less than two feet.

"I guess you couldn't write a better script," Earnhardt Jr. said. "I think that was the way it was supposed to be at this point in my career and at this point in his career. . . . I was trying with all of my might to win that race, but that's storybook right there."

Earnhardt wasn't about to give his son any quarter.

"He's going to have to earn everything just like his dad did," Earnhardt said. "I don't think he would have wanted me to let him win. He would have gone home and everybody would have said, 'Your dad let you win.' That wouldn't have been cool."

If practicing on the track in Japan had been better than winning his first Busch title, that IROC finish at Michigan had to be better than winning a second straight.

"I was a rookie so I guess it was all right if I had lost the championship last year," Earnhardt Jr. said. "But we won the championship last year and we were supposed to perform like champions this year."

Earnhardt Jr. did that. He won six Busch races in 1999 and clinched the championship at Phoenix with one race to go.

With two championships in two full seasons in the Busch Series, Earnhardt Jr. was ready for the next move — the biggest one a stock-car driver ever takes.

GIANT *steps*

There were times during the 1999 season when Dale Earnhardt Jr. felt like a twig being swept along in a raging river.

All of the excitement and interest in his rise to stock-car stardom provided great opportunities for him, on and off the track, but those opportunities brought responsibilities and obligations. And with so many people pulling at him in so many different directions, Earnhardt Jr. sometimes found himself scheduled to be in two places at once.

He was trying to keep all of his sponsors and fans happy, but he was also trying to win a second Busch Series title and get his feet under him for the move into Winston Cup in 2000. It was, at least for a while, a mighty struggle.

As the year went by, however, Earnhardt Jr. and the people working with him began to get a better handle on the demands being placed on his time. His second-half surge toward the successful defense of his Busch championship indicated he'd begun to come to terms with the demands his stardom were just beginning to place on him.

Expectations were unquestionably high for his rookie season in Winston Cup. Earnhardt Jr. and Matt Kenseth, who'd battled for two seasons in the Busch Series, were moving up together. Tony Stewart, who'd dazzled the Winston Cup circuit with three wins as a rookie in 1999, predicted the 2000 rookies would quickly make people forget about what he'd accomplished in his first season.

But Earnhardt Jr. didn't win the Daytona 500 to start his rookie season. He started second at Atlanta and led the race, but his No. 8 Chevrolet shot suddenly up into the wall. He finished 29th in

Expectations were unquestionably high for his rookie season in Winston Cup.

a race his father won in a side-by-side finish with Bobby Labonte, giving Earnhardt his 75th career win.

Earnhardt Jr. started 10th at Darlington and wrecked again, finishing 40th. He wrecked again at Bristol the next weekend, too. There were explanations for those wrecks — a cut brake fluid line leaking at Atlanta, a stripped axle at Darlington — but it was still hard for him not to wonder if, perhaps, he might be in over his head. Had he tried to make the move to Cup too soon?

His father, his team, his friends and just about anybody else he talked to told him no. Their confidence helped keep him from getting down on himself. So, too, did his consistently good qualifying efforts. When he qualified fourth for the DirecTV 500 at Texas Motor Speedway, it was the seventh straight race he'd started in the first six rows.

Earnhardt Jr. had earned his first career Busch Series win at Texas, so he knew the potential was there for a good day. He was in the lead by Lap 17 and at one point later in the race pulled away to lead by more than six seconds over his nearest challenger. At times, he wondered if his car was really that good, or whether other drivers were just waiting to show all their cards.

In the second half of the race, several cars tried two-tire changes on pit stops to gain track position. Tony Eury Sr. stayed with his strategy all day long, however, changing four tires and keeping his driver calm. On Lap 282, Earnhardt Jr. passed DEI teammate Steve Park for the lead and never gave it up again. He pulled away and took the checkered flag nearly six seconds ahead of second-place Jeff Burton.

"Woooooooooooooooooooo!" Earnhardt Jr. screamed over the radio after winning in just his 12th career start.

Just as he had been when Earnhardt Jr. got his first Busch Series win, Earnhardt was there when the No. 8 car got to victory lane. He leaned in the window for a quick father-son talk before Earnhardt Jr. began his celebration.

"He just told me he loved me and he wanted to make sure I took the time to enjoy this," Earnhardt Jr. said. "You can get so swept up with what's going on around

you that you don't really enjoy it yourself personally, so he just wanted me to take a minute and do this and celebrate how I wanted to celebrate."

Earnhardt also told his son to find another ride home — Earnhardt wasn't planning to keep his jet waiting until Earnhardt Jr. was through with the post-race interviews.

"You never really do know if you're going to win — ever," Earnhardt Jr. said. "Guys race and race and race for years and years and years and don't win races. This here is awesome, man, just incredible."

The incredible moments would keep on coming for Earnhardt Jr.

At Richmond in early May, he survived a pit-road bump with Stewart late in the race and went on to pass Earnhardt for the lead with 31 laps to go on his way to his second win.

In the days before The Winston at Charlotte, Lowe's Motor Speedway's president, H.A. "Humpy" Wheeler, who'd known Earnhardt Jr. since he was just a boy, predicted that the sport's hot young star would win the all-star race. Earnhardt didn't like the pick at all, telling Wheeler he was putting too much pressure on the rookie.

"But Dale," Wheeler said, "I think he's going to win!"

And he did, giving him a chance to really celebrate with his father. They were at Charlotte, so Earnhardt had no plane to catch. He came to the victory celebration and shared the crowd's cheers with Earnhardt Jr.

"I could have quit driving race cars for the rest of my life and been happy," Earnhardt Jr. would say later. "At that very moment I felt like I would never enjoy another win as much as I enjoyed that feeling I was having. Dad and I threw beer around on each other and jumped around and hollered and made fools of ourselves on national television. It was a lot of fun."

Earnhardt Jr. and his team never did find the magic again that year, however, and an inconsistent performance in the season's second half allowed Kenseth, who got his first win at Charlotte the weekend after Earnhardt Jr.'s win in The Winston, to win Winston Cup rookie-of-the-year honors.

The late-season dip bothered Earnhardt Jr. He and his crew sometimes found themselves pointing fingers at one another, arguing about who was to blame for the problems instead of figuring out how to fix them.

When the season ended, however, they sat back and looked at what they'd done. They'd won two races plus The Winston and had earned more than $2.8 million. Despite the problems they'd finished 16th in points, certainly respectable if not up to the team's lofty expectations.

Most important, however, the team had established for itself a firm foothold

in NASCAR's top division, building on its success from the Busch Series. Earnhardt Jr. was already among the most popular drivers in the sport, and the promise he showed fueled his fame.

After one season in Winston Cup, Earnhardt Jr. was a star. What's more, his success seemed to rekindle the competitive fires in his father. Earnhardt finished second in the 2000 standings to Bobby Labonte, and looked ahead to 2001 for a chance to win a record eighth championship.

A new century was about to begin. Sadly, however, an era was also about to end.

farewell, SUPERMAN

"I thought he was Superman," Dale Jr. would later say about his father. "I thought he was invincible."

In December 2000, Dale Earnhardt Jr. had a dream about the 2001 Daytona 500.

"I was out front all day," he said of the dream. "I kept telling myself I won it in my second time in the race."

His father had won the 500 in 1998 and was the acclaimed master of racing on NASCAR's restrictor-plate tracks. But Earnhardt wasn't part of Earnhardt Jr.'s dream.

"Dad," he would say a month before Daytona, "wasn't there."

He always had been, of course, at least as long as Earnhardt Jr. had been racing. And of all the things the seven-time champion's son had wanted to achieve in the sport, earning his father's respect was right at the top of that list.

"It's like a never-ending process, earning his respect," Earnhardt Jr. said. "It's bottomless. I get worn out by it at times.

But it's something you always want. Sometimes it becomes more important than the job at hand.

"What other reason do you race for? You race for thousands of dollars. That's good. You race to win. That's good. Those are good reasons. But there's nothing wrong with wanting to make my dad happy."

One year into his Winston Cup career, Earnhardt Jr. had already begun to learn some valuable lessons.

"When I was 10 or 15 years old, I would sit there and watch Dad race and think, 'Man, he gets to do that for a living and gets paid for doing it,'" Earnhardt Jr. said. "I never thought about all of those things he had to do off the track. It is a job, and a lot of responsibilities come along with it.

"As time went on, I slowly started to realize some of those things. Thank God I

had him to kind of take some notes off of and pay attention to."

There had already been some memorable moments for the father and son on the track. The exhibition race in Japan, for one, and the door-to-door battle in the IROC race at Michigan for another.

When Earnhardt won the Daytona 500 in 1998, a group of family and friends gathered long after midnight at the airport back in North Carolina to welcome him home and celebrate the victory. When Earnhardt Jr. got his first Cup win at Texas, Earnhardt made sure a similar group was there to welcome Earnhardt Jr. home that night, too.

In February of 2001, a week before Earnhardt Jr.'s second Cup season would begin, the Earnhardts finally got a chance to race with each other — as opposed to against each other. Chevrolet gave Earnhardt and Earnhardt Jr. a chance to race in a

Corvette in the Rolex 24-hour race at Daytona with Andy Pilgrim and Kelly Collins as part of a two-team factory effort in America's most prestigious endurance event.

The Earnhardts' car finished fourth overall and second in their class to the other Corvette, which was the overall winning car in the race. Earnhardt and Earnhardt Jr. had a wonderful time, gushing about how much they'd enjoyed the experience and talking about how they'd love to do it again.

But they would never get the chance.

On Feb. 18, 2001, on the final lap of the Daytona 500, Earnhardt hit the Turn 4 wall just as Earnhardt Jr. was chasing DEI teammate Michael Waltrip under the checkered flag. It was Waltrip's first victory in a Winston Cup points race in his first race for DEI, and it should have been a happy day for the Earnhardts' team and for the family.

But as the post-race festivities began, race fans began to notice that something was very wrong down on the bottom of the high-banked fourth turn at the track where Earnhardt had won more races than any other driver in history. Emergency workers were scrambling around the black No. 3 Chevrolet, fighting a desperate battle. Earnhardt Jr. climbed out of his car and began running in that direction, sensing that something was terribly, terribly wrong.

Earnhardt's car had broken loose between turns 3 and 4, shooting up the track toward the outside wall. An eye blink before it hit the wall, the No. 3 Monte Carlo was hit in the side by Ken Schrader's Pontiac, turning it slightly so that the car hit the concrete barrier at an extremely critical angle. All of the forces in the high-speed crash were working together in the worst possible way.

When Earnhardt's car finally came to rest, Schrader's stopped nearby. Schrader jumped out and went to help his fellow driver. He looked inside the No. 3 Chevrolet and quickly began motioning for the ambulance crews to come quickly.

And then he turned away.

The medical crews began working on Earnhardt within a few seconds, and continued their efforts as he was taken from the track and to a hospital just down International Speedway Boulevard. Their efforts to revive him were futile, however.

"I thought he was Superman," Earnhardt Jr. would later say about his father. "I thought he was invincible."

Dale Earnhardt, one of the greatest drivers in NASCAR history, had suffered a basal skull fracture. The blow to his head had been instantly fatal.

As Earnhardt Jr. had dreamed, when the Daytona 500 ended his dad wasn't there.

LIKE FATHER, *like son*

Even for people who knew, or at least thought they knew, how big NASCAR had become, the scope of the reaction to Dale Earnhardt's death was a surprise.

In the days following the seven-time champion's passing, thousands upon thousands of fans found their way to the DEI headquarters in Mooresville to pay their respects. A memorial service held in Charlotte four days after his death was televised nationally, and fans in communities all around the country arranged and attended services and gatherings of their own to share their feelings and express their grief.

In the midst of all that, the Earnhardt family and the people at Dale Earnhardt Inc. knew one thing for certain. Earnhardt had built DEI to continue his legacy after his racing days were done, and now the

task of keeping that purpose alive had fallen to them.

Dale Earnhardt Jr. raced at Rockingham a week after his father's death, but crashed his Chevrolet into the Turn 3 wall on the first lap of the race. Teammate Steve Park, however, completed a rain-delayed victory the following day to show how determined DEI was to keep on going.

When he went back to Texas Motor Speedway, a year after that first Winston Cup victory, Earnhardt Jr. first began to show signs he was getting his wheels back under him on the track by winning the pole and running well.

"It will be a long, long time before I feel like I felt before all of that happened," Earnhardt Jr. said. "I think about him all of the time. ... Just when you

At the 2001 Pepsi 400, another driver named Earnhardt showed he had picked up a few pointers from the old man.

think you might be feeling better about it and things are getting easier, you'll hit a bump in the road and you'll spend two or three days when you can't think about anything else."

Earnhardt Jr. said he was becoming a different person.

"I had this little bit of a little brat in me somewhere," he said. "That's all gone. The way I look at racing ... , the way I feel about going to the track, ... the way I prepare myself for each race is totally different. Some of the aspects of racing that were huge to me a year ago don't really matter anymore. Then there are things I didn't ever think I would appreciate that I do."

As the 2001 season continued, few people in NASCAR knew exactly what they would feel like when they made their return trip to Daytona for July's Pepsi 400. And nobody could put themselves in Earnhardt Jr.'s shoes, anticipating what it would be like the first time he drove into the infield and looked out at Turn 4, where his father's crash had happened just a few months before.

Earnhardt Jr. took the challenge head-on. He went to Daytona a day early and went over to where the Feb. 18 accident had taken place. He sat there and thought about his father, about what it had meant to be with him on the race track and about what it now meant to be out there without him. He thought about all of the things Earnhardt had tried to teach him and about how much sense a lot of those things were starting to make.

Tony Eury Sr. and his crew had been working on the car they'd bring for him to drive that weekend, knowing how important this race would be for their driver. They did their work well, too, for when the No. 8 Chevrolet carrying a special Major League Baseball-theme paint scheme got on the track, it flew like a Nolan Ryan fastball.

Earnhardt Jr. led much of the race, but after making a four-tire pit stop on a late-race yellow he found himself seventh on a restart with six laps to go. It took him just two to get back into the lead. He got the top spot by passing Johnny Benson going into Turn 4, just a few feet away from the spot where his father had wrecked five months earlier.

"Man, I just don't know what to say," Earnhardt Jr. said after pulling his car into the trioval grass and beginning an emotional celebration right there, right where Earnhardt had cut celebratory doughnuts after the 1998 win in the 500, with the cheers of 150,000 fans showering around him. "I don't know how I did it. Dad was with me tonight."

Michael Waltrip, who'd won the ill-fated Daytona 500 in February, had fought his way up to second at the checkered flag. He pulled his No. 15 Chevrolet alongside Earnhardt Jr.'s in the trioval and joined the emotional celebration.

No driver has won more races at Daytona and Talladega than Earnhardt. It is part of his legend that he could "see the air" that is so important in how cars race in the aerodynamic draft at those two huge tracks, and it was absolutely true that nobody knew more about how to use that draft to his advantage than Earnhardt did.

On that Saturday night in July 2001, however, another driver named Earnhardt showed he had picked up a few pointers from the old man. The highest compliment anyone could pay Earnhardt Jr. was that, in winning the Pepsi 400, he drove just like his dad.

In a van riding to his post-race news conference, Earnhardt Jr. looked over at Tony Eury Sr. "We don't know just how huge this is," Earnhardt Jr. said.

It was a remarkable story, too remarkable for some. Over the next few days, Earnhardt Jr. would face questions from skeptics who believed his emotional, storybook triumph was the product of some NASCAR-orchestrated conspiracy. The only evidence anyone had was Earnhardt Jr.'s dominance of the race, but that didn't stop the questions.

"A reporter came up and asked me that. I came as close as I ever have to knocking him straight out," Earnhardt Jr. said. "I just couldn't believe it. ... I mean, aside from the days that I had my father with me, that was the greatest day of my life. I just can't believe people would step on it like that."

the need TO SUCCEED

Emotional victories became a Dale Earnhardt Jr. specialty in 2001.

After his incredible win at Daytona in July, Earnhardt Jr. next visited victory lane in September at Dover, less than two weeks after the Sept. 11 terrorist attacks on America. It was NASCAR's first race since that awful day, and after a moving display of patriotism and national fortitude before the green flag, Earnhardt Jr. carried the Stars and Stripes around the 1-mile Dover track on a reverse victory lap following his win.

"I don't think it mattered who would have won this race," Earnhardt Jr. said. "The fact that we're here and doing it, we're driving and racing and the fans could witness a good race, that was healing enough. I was just really glad and fortunate to have been the guy."

In October at Talladega, Earnhardt Jr. won again, furthering the Earnhardt family's rich history in restrictor-plate racing.

One year earlier, his father had rallied dramatically from 18th to first with five laps to go in what would turn out to be his final career victory. Earnhardt Jr. found himself 13th with 33 laps to go this time, and passed Bobby Labonte on the final lap to get his third victory of the season and the fifth of his career.

Earnhardt Jr. finished his second season eighth in the final standings, eight spots better than he'd done as a rookie. He was maturing as a racer and as a person, and his team was growing right along with him. He marched into 2002 looking forward to continuing that improvement and building on the foundation he'd put down in those sometimes difficult first two seasons.

He started the year with a flourish, winning the season's first Busch Series race at Daytona in a No. 3 Chevrolet owned by Richard Childress, his father's car owner. He finished second in the Bud

As Earnhardt Jr. gains experience and grows as a racer, he has his sights set on joining his father on the list of the sport's winners.

Shootout and seemed to have a car strong enough to win the Daytona 500 before problems ended that dream.

Earnhardt Jr. did get his sixth career win at Talladega, adding another notch to his restrictor-plate racing belt. He also won over even more fans in The Winston all-star race at Charlotte when he backed off rookie Ryan Newman's car when Newman got loose less than two laps from the finish after a charging Earnhardt Jr. had nudged him from behind.

Earnhardt Jr. could have wrecked Newman and won the all-star race, but he made the split-second decision not to. Would his hard-charging father, "The Intimidator," have made the same instinctive decision? Perhaps not.

Earnhardt Jr. brushed aside the praise he got for not taking Newman out, admitting he wasn't sure if he backed off because he didn't want to wreck the rookie or because he thought the rookie was already wrecking. Still, the way Earnhardt Jr. handled the entire affair was yet another sign of how rapidly he had matured.

Image is a funny thing. Some people see Earnhardt Jr. come into the garage wearing blue jeans and a rock band's T-shirt under the perpetually backward baseball cap and see a marketing strategy.

To be certain, Earnhardt Jr. has a public persona that is a little less country and a little more rock 'n' roll than many of the sport's older stars. He has been interviewed by Rolling Stone and Playboy magazines and was a presenter on the "MTV Movie Awards". He has an endorsement deal with Drakkar Noir, a line of men's fragrances sold in the finest stores. His book about his rookie season, called "Driver #8" and co-written by Jade Gurss, made the best-seller lists and is one of the most successful sports books in recent history.

Because of that, Earnhardt Jr. in many ways personifies a new image for NASCAR racing. Strong ratings for network TV coverage and other signs of stock-car racing's ability to buck a trend of declining interest in American professional sports have propelled NASCAR to a much higher profile nationwide, and Earnhardt Jr.'s popularity is helping to fuel that rise.

That's fine with Earnhardt Jr. He handles the crowds seeking his autograph and pushing for a moment of his time while also dealing with the responsibilities of driving his race car and helping his stepmother, Teresa Earnhardt, guide the future direction of DEI.

He still surfs the Internet and likes to sleep late. He still likes to hang out with his buddies, often in the basement of the

house he built on Earnhardt's land not far from the trailer where he lived just a few years ago. Earnhardt Jr. turned that basement into his own nightclub, complete with floor-to-ceiling speakers, and nicknamed it "Club E." In the past year, however, he's redone things and turned a place where he and his pals used to party into a place where they now more often just chill out.

Earnhardt Jr. turns 28 on Oct. 10. He's thinking more these days about where he someday wants to be and how he intends to get there.

"When my dad was here I could just about do whatever I wanted to and get away with it," Earnhardt Jr. said. "I always had him to fall back on.

"Now I don't have anything to fall back on except how I do it. It's going to reflect on me instead of my father. Before, if I didn't do something right it was his fault.

"One thing I've learned…is that you

have to make yourself happy first. I will change. There will be a day when I want to get married and have a little son I can take to the race track. There will be a day when I want to take some more time for myself.

I will make some decisions that not everybody might like, but I think people will just have to understand that. … I've only got one life, it's not like I can do it over again. So I am going to do it like I want to."

Earnhardt Jr. says the advice his father gave him is more important to him now than ever before. He also has the same fire burning inside. As Earnhardt Jr. gains experience and he grows as a racer, he has his sights set on joining his father on the list of the sport's winners.

"My heart has always wanted it, but now I feel it's more of a reality," Earnhardt Jr. said. "I feel like I can be a champion."

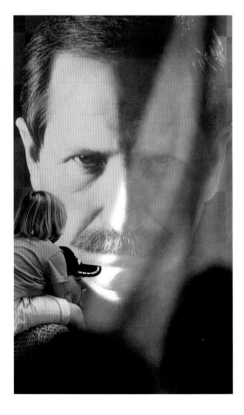